CHEETAHS

Wildlife Monographs - Cheetahs
Copyright © 2004 Evans Mitchell Books

Text and photography copyright © 2004 ARWP Ltd

Dr. Tracey Rich and Andy Rouse have asserted their rights
to be identified as the author and photographer of this work in
accordance with Section 77 of the Copyright, Designs and
Patents Act 1988

First published in Great Britain by
Evans Mitchell Books
Norfolk Court
1, Norfolk Road
Rickmansworth
Herts. WD3 1 LA
United Kingdom

Jacket and book design by
Sunita Gahir
Big Metal Fish Design Services
bigmetalfish.com

Maps by Mark Franklin

British Library Cataloguing in Publication Data. A CIP record of
this book is available on request from the British Library.

ISBN: 1-901268-09-8

10 9 8 7 6 5 4 3 2 1

Printed and bound in Hong Kong

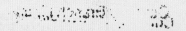

CHEETAHS

DR. TRACEY RICH & ANDY ROUSE

Evans Mitchell Books

CONTENTS

FOREWORD

Wildlife Monographs — Cheetahs is a visually stunning book, beautifully photographed, on one of the Earth's most endangered and very special animal species.

The photographer and zoologist Dr. Tracey Rich and wildlife photographer Andy Rouse, show the cheetah in its natural habitat and portray its struggle for survival. As well as documenting its long history on earth, this informative book brings together all the known facts about the cheetah in a realistic fashion. The highly informative text is supported by a wealth of high-quality, beautiful photographs of cheetahs, presenting the behaviour, landscapes and habitats of cheetahs where they still roam.

Tracey and Andy are to be congratulated on their achievement. It will be through such shared knowledge and conservation efforts that the cheetah may have a chance to survive. As a result, I am sure that readers will be inspired to do something themselves in order to help this endangered species survive for future generations. I hope this book will continue to be a very worthwhile resource about cheetahs for many years to come.

LAURIE MARKER, PhD
Founder and Executive Director
Cheetah Conservation Fund

INTRODUCTION

With a worldwide reputation for being the fastest land mammal, the cheetah is one of the most highly specialised of Africa's big cats. Long and sleek, but lacking the wanton look of a fearsome predator such as the lion or leopard, cheetahs are one of the big cat species most often overlooked on the African plains. Yet the cheetah is in trouble. Classified as an endangered species, it is under threat of extinction as a result of loss of natural habitat and pressures from an ever- increasing human population. In addition, it suffers from a natural lack of genetic diversity.

Wildlife Monographs – Cheetahs provides a privileged glimpse of the lives of cheetahs in Africa today, courtesy of the wonderful imagery of internationally renown professional wildlife photographers Andy Rouse and Tracey Rich.

RIGHT: The cheetah is one of the most specialised of Africa's big cats and holds the record for being the fastest land mammal.

ABOVE: Despite the cheetah's supremacy in terms of speed they are one of the world's most endangered big cats.

LEFT: The cheetah is tall, slim and graceful with distinctive markings ideally suited to the niche it occupies in the savannah ecosystem.

Highlighting the magnificence of this most ancient of big cats, we will see how extremely specialised the cheetah has become on the African plains and what a predicament the animal is currently facing. Accompanying cheetah families on the ground and at key stages in their lives, we will witness the truly awesome adaptation of this creature to its niche in the savannah ecosystem.

Come with us as we explore the world of the enigmatic cheetah, view special moments from some of their lives and explore some ways in which experts are helping to conserve this precious animal.

HISTORY & DISTRIBUTION

The cheetah must rank as one of the most ancient of big cat predators. Currently believed to have originated in North America before the last Ice Age, the cheetah we know today, Acinonyx jubatus, was just one of several cheetah-like cats roaming the Earth. Cheetahs once prowled

LEFT: One of the world's most ancient of big cats: there were many varieties of cheetah-like species in the past.

BELOW: Cheetahs once hunted across four different continents.

the open plains and wastelands of four continents - Africa, Asia, Europe and North America - being widely dispersed, from the Cape of Good Hope through to the Mediterranean, the Arabian peninsula, the Middle East, India and the southern areas of the former Soviet Union.

At the onset of the last Ice Age (about 10 thousand years ago), some cheetah species migrated towards the warmer regions of the Earth

LEFT: The cheetah became specialised at hunting in vast tracts of savannah grassland.

RIGHT AND ABOVE: The range of the cheetah was restricted through changes in climate due to the last Ice Age.

namely, Africa and Asia. Other species were unable to survive in the changing climate and sadly died out in the process of evolution. Those remaining survived in reduced numbers and with a contracting range in which to live. They were forced to breed with closely related individuals, creating a genetic bottleneck. In doing so, the genetic diversity of the species was diminished, meaning that they became more susceptible to disease, illness, deformities, poor reproduction and high mortality rates. The lack of genetic diversity makes

ABOVE: The process of evolution has caused the cheetah to become inbred and pass through a genetic bottleneck.

WORLD CHEETAH DISTRIBUTION

Cheetahs

ABOVE: With a lack of genetic diversity, the cheetah, as a species, has an overall poor survival rate.

a species of animal less able to survive changes in its environment. In most mammal species, individuals share approximately 80 per cent of their genetic make-up. In contrast, in cheetahs this figure rises to around 99 per cent.

In conjunction with changes due to human activity occurring at a far faster rate than would have occurred in the natural process of evolution, this has meant the survival of the cheetah became threatened.

Today, the world-wide population of *Acinonyx jubatus* is thought to be in the region of 12,500 and these are found in widely dispersed, small isolated pockets in Africa with very few remaining in Iran.

The 'critically endangered' cheetah is listed under Appendix I of the 1973 Convention on International Trade in Endangered Species of Wild Flora and Fauna (CITES), meaning that it is under threat of extinction.

RIGHT AND BELOW: The cheetah's stronghold remains in savannah and semi-arid habitats of sub-Saharan Africa.

DISTINGUISHING FEATURES

Cheetahs are characterised by a unique look. Relatively thin, with long legs, a very long tail, small ears and spotted coat, the cheetah gives the appearance of being relatively fragile in comparison to, say, a muscular lion or heavyweight leopard - some of the other big cats that share the African savannah alongside the cheetah.

BELOW: Built for speed, the cheetah has a similar conformation to a greyhound.

RIGHT: They have distinctive faces with black teardrop markings below the eyes.

ABOVE: Deep amber coloured eyes and small rounded ears are characteristic of a cheetah.

LEFT: They have forfeited powerful weapons and muscles for lightness and speed.

ABOVE: A long muscular tail acts as a rudder and braking system when travelling at high speeds.

The cheetah's overall conformation is designed for speed and has been replicated by Man's selective breeding of dogs like the greyhound, whippet and Afghan hound, which also have a similar look.

The cheetah's coat is the colour of straw covered with small black solid spots. The belly is lighter, sometimes white in colour. They have large wide eyes, amber in colouration and defined by black teardrop-shaped outlines running down the face to the mouth. The cheetah has forfeited the powerful weapons of other predators for speed and it possesses weak jaws and small teeth in comparison.

It has low set ears that sit almost in line with the top of the head. Black ear tips are noticeable on the rear of the ears and are used in communication. A long tail ends in a large lobe, banded in black and white. The tail is muscular and acts as a stabiliser, or rudder, controlling the cat's direction and speed at high speeds.

The feet are armed with non-retractable claws unlike those of domestic cats. In effect, these slightly blunted claws work like studded or spiked sports shoes, allowing the animal far greater grip and traction on the ground when running at high speed. The exception is the dew claw located a little way up the foreleg. This is pointed and sharp and used to hook the prey animal when running.

ABOVE LEFT: A cheetah's coat is the colour of straw with defined solid black spots.

LEFT: Cheetahs have non-retractable claws for enhanced grip when running.

RIGHT: In comparison with other predators, the cheetah has relatively small jaws and teeth.

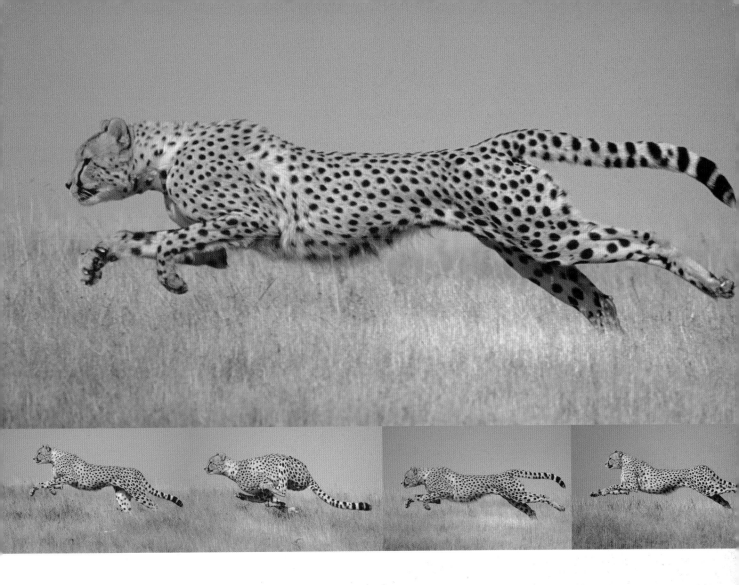

LEFT AND ABOVE: To achieve the speed required to bring down their prey, the cheetah is a lightweight big cat. A flexible spine and hips allow the cheetah's stride to reach in excess of 7 metres.

The cheetah has a small, rounded head, a short neck and a highly flexible back that appears to sway at walk, but which flexes dramatically when at speed. The hips and shoulders are able to swivel around the spine allowing the cat to extend and contract its body and achieve strides of 7- 8m (23 – 26ft). Running, it can reach a top speed of 90-112kph (60-70mph).

A cheetah stands between 70-90 cm (about 28 – 35in) tall at the shoulder. Males weigh in at around 50kg (110.2lbs) on average with female

being lighter at an average of 40kg (about 90 lbs). Females also appear lighter framed and less robust than males.

ABOVE: Unlike other big cats, cheetahs are built for speed and are light and slim.

LEFT: Cheetahs have great eyesight and constantly scan their environment.

RIGHT: Fitting perfectly in their environment, the cheetah's coat is the colour of dried grasses.

ABOVE AND RIGHT: Forward facing eyes are a distinguishing feature of a predator: the cheetah is no exception.

 # HABITAT & DIET

Cheetahs are designed to hunt gazelles, with their favourites species in East African habitats being the Thomson (*Gazella thomsonii*) and Grant's gazelle (*Gazella granti*). They also favour hares, which comprise a significant part of their diet when they are unable to catch gazelle.

BELOW AND LEFT: The cheetah's favourite prey are gazelles: they have a variety of hunting techniques.

The optimum cheetah hunting habitat is slightly different to that of the leopard and the lion, but often occurs in a similar area, as prey move around their feeding grounds. Being adapted for speed, the cheetah needs open plains absent of any physical obstacles which may lead to a disastrous fall or prevent it from out running its prey. However, hunting in a completely open space is also unsuitable, as the cheetah needs some cover – usually in the form of bushes and medium-length grass – in order to get within striking distance of its prey before they become alerted to the cheeetah's presence.

In slightly more wooded areas, cheetah are still able to hunt, so long as there are sufficient open areas to run and they have a good chance of over-coming their prey. In these types of habitat, mostly in southern Africa, other types of gazelle and antelope are hunted such as the Impala (*Aepyceros melampus*). Single cheetahs are seldom able to take prey larger than themselves but when working in cooperation with others can bring down most prey

animals including on rare occasions zebra (*Equus burchelli*), the lion's favourite food item.

To catch its prey, a cheetah has to overtake the chosen individual in order that it may trip the prey animal's front legs with a swipe of its forepaws. This will usually bring the gazelle crashing to the ground, potentially crippling it in the process. The cheetah is so highly specialised at running fast, one of the reasons why it is unable to sustain prolonged periods of running is due to the physiological constraint of heat loss. Running fast causes humans to sweat, but like canids, felines are unable to do this. Instead they must lose excess heat by other means, such aspanting behaviour. Obviously, a cheetah cannot pant and run at the same time. Although it has specialised heat exchanging tissues at the base of its brain to stop it overheating, a cheetah must stop running when the brain's temperature surpasses a specified threshold. As a result, a cheetah needs to calculate accurately the energy needs of a potential chase in order to prevent it from overheating before it reaches striking distance.

RIGHT: Cheetahs are predators meaning that they kill other animals for food.

Consequently, a cheetah's hunt needs to occur with around 300m (312yd) , start to finish, before it has to abandon its hunt.

A cheetah has a very well defined pattern of behaviour when hunting. Firstly, it will need to find a vantage point from which to observe the potential prey and assess which individual is likely to be the focus of its attention. To do this, cheetahs will climb termite mounds, raised areas of ground and trees or bushes with relatively low branches to gain a height advantage and a panoramic view of the surroundings. It will often traverse the local area assessing the situation from various angles before deciding on a plan of action. Interestingly, some animals have learned to utilise the intrusion of tourist vehicles in their habitat to their own advantage, using them either as mobile termite mounds or as cover in order to get closer to their prey and increase their chances of a successful hunt. Cheetahs, at this point of the hunt, have various strategies available to them enabling them to get closer to their prey and to get crucially within striking distance of them - 50m (54yd).

The most familiar way of hunting by a cheetah, especially where there is sufficient cover, is to stalk as near to the prey as possible before launching an

explosive burst of speed directed at a pre-chosen individual. Stalking is an extremely well defined behaviour and takes no account of wind direction. The cheetah will walk in a crouched position head and back slung as low as possible below the grasses, the tips of the shoulder blades the highest point. The cheetah will freeze motionless and will even lie down or sit hunched in the grass should the prey look up and give indications of having detected its presence. The stalk usually lasts for a few minutes but may last for anything up to an hour under difficult circumstances.

RIGHT: To avoid the unwanted attentions of competitors, the cheetah will drag its prey to the safety and shade of a nearby bush.

LEFT: A successful hunt usually involves an explosive turn of speed.

The cheetah when it strikes usually reaches speeds on average of 64kph (40mph), despite the fact that it can run at speeds approaching double this. Gazelles, however, have an interesting tactic that they employ in order to escape their hunter, even from a cheetah that has already overtaken them. Gazelles are extremely nimble and are able to perform abrupt twists and turns at high speed. This ability makes it difficult for the cheetah to catch them when running so fast in a straight line. Frequently, a cheetah will be exhausted through the extra exertion of turning before it can bring the gazelle down by a swift hook of the front legs with its forepaw. The kill itself occurs by a swift bite to the windpipe, usually approached from behind thus avoiding potential injury from flailing hooves. The vice-like grip continues until the prey has ceased struggling, which may take around 4 and a half minutes.

ABOVE: A cheetah drags its prey to safety before starting to eat. It can be an exhausting task.

In other circumstances, especially where there is little cover and the cheetah is in need of a meal or has young to feed, a cheetah may behave in what appears to be a very strange way. The cheetah walks confidently straight towards its chosen herd of gazelle who may be already alert to its presence. However, it is the point at which the herd decides to take flight that is the important factor here. If it is within 60-70m (some 66 – 77 yards), then the cheetah is in with a chance of a kill. Fleeing prey animals appear to stimulate cheetah to pursue them. Galloping the first few metres before launching into an all out sprint, the cheetah has a chance of a strike.

ABOVE: Cheetahs are not particularly successful hunters. Running at high speed is physically exhausting and this limits their ability to sustain a hunt.

RIGHT: It is unusual to see cheetahs drinking.

Other hunting strategies include galloping at full speed straight at an unsuspecting prey herd in the hope of getting within striking distance before the prey has detected it and begun fleeing and/or the cheetah has over-heated. Another, is to simply sit and wait until the prey herd move to within striking distance from resting position.

Despite so many different hunting strategies, which are modified according to the specific situation, the cheetah is not as successful a hunter as one may expect. Less than half of its hunting attempts are successful. Following an unsuccessful one, it may have to wait in the region of half-an-hour before it can try again, needing to cool down and regain its breath. The cheetah's breathing rate will increase from 60 to 150 a minute during a chase.

Cheetahs have a much higher success rate hunting fawns but a popular misconception is they will take animals in poor condition or ill. Cheetahs will consume approximately 14kg (31 lbs) of meat in one gazelle kill, and it is unlikely that the cheetah will hunt again for another 2-5 days after, unless the meal was small or it has other mouths to feed. It is unusual to see cheetahs drinking for they can go for several days without water, however, when needed the cats will travel between 5-10km (3.1 – 6.2 miles) in order to access fresh water.

In the evolutionary race to become the fastest cat on the plains and to exploit an available niche in the ecosystem, cheetah have sacrificed the power and weapons retained by other big cat predators such as the lion and leopard. This puts the cheetah at a disadvantage in terms of being able to defend itself from competitors. Cheetahs are usually the first animal to run away or surrender to others whether or not they pose a direct threat to them or their kill. Up to 10 per cent of their kills may be lost to lions, hyenas, leopards and even wild dogs.

Even when cheetah have successfully hunted, they have to defend their kill from the threat of other animals and birds.

For this reason they do not return to their kill, unlike other cats. They are quick to feed, gulping down their kill as quickly as they can to avoid detection by competitors, sometimes this means eating their prey in the blazing heat of the day on the open plain but if possible the cheetah will drag the carcass to the shade of a bush or tree. The cat's cryptic colouration will help it remain undetected until it has had its fill.

SOCIAL STRUCTURE & COMMUNICATION

Cheetahs are dependent upon the location and movements of their prey. Their home range can vary widely, depending on the nature of their prey species and, in turn, upon the prey's dependence on localised rainfall and grass growth. Ranges may vary from 50-65sq km (19 - 25sq miles) to over 1000sq km (about 386sq miles) for females. In general, females outnumber male cheetah in the wild by two to one. Males tend to roam far wider and will range over vast distances when they are initially seeking to acquire a territory for themselves. Transient males follow a high-risk strategy, as they face considerable danger from other established cheetah territory holders, which are intolerant of intruders. Cheetahs rarely exhibit aggression towards one another and tend to avoid conflict. However, occasional fights do occur, especially around oestrus females. The consequences can be severe and may even result in death.

Once established, a male cheetah maintains a territory covering an area far smaller than that of

RIGHT: The cheetah's home range depends upon the availability of resources such as food, water and potential mates.

ABOVE: Coalitions of male cheetahs tend to be very successful and are usually littermates.

LEFT: Male cheetahs tend to become territorial, whilst females range over a wider area.

OVERLEAF: A single male cheetah holding a territory is more likely to be the sire of the offspring of a female he mates with.

a females home range, which is unusual in cats. The area may cover between 40 - 80sq km (about 15 – 31sq miles) and territories are fiercely defended, with little overlap occurring between neighbouring male territories. However, male territories and female home ranges do overlap, ensuring that females can access males and their defended resources.

Male cheetahs may live alone, in pairs or (less frequently) in trios, depending upon localised conditions and access to resources, including females. It is thought that single male cheetahs find it harder to keep and maintain a territory compared to those in coalitions, but that being single has a greater chance of siring the offspring of females mated with.

Coalitions are an interesting phenomenon and also occur in lion populations. Male cheetahs that form part of a coalition are usually littermates. Female littermates are the first to leave the family group as they approach sexual maturity and after

this rarely have contact with each other. Male cheetahs in a coalition are not particularly social and rarely lie or sleep together. Close contact between individuals, such as greeting ceremonies, are limited. Scent marking and defence of the territory is performed collectively.

Despite often being found in groups, cheetahs generally remain solitary animals, with groups tending to be mothers and juvenile off spring or closely related siblings.

Most unusually, in Namibia, where the majority of farmland has been fenced and other predators exterminated, cheetahs may form groups comprised of various combinations of sexes (usually littermates) where their coalitions are able to take bigger prey such as kudu (*Tragelaphus spp.*) through active cooperation.

The cheetahs on the African savannah occupy a very specialised niche in the hierarchy of big cats. Both in social structure and prey base, they fall somewhere between lions and leopards. Lions are specialists of the savannah, working in teams and usually going for larger game species such as zebra. The leopard is an impala specialist and hangs around trees and bushy areas with ambush being their main hunting technique.

The cheetah is a diurnal creature having peaks of activity at either end of the day, when the weather is at its coolest. Big cats of all descriptions

ABOVE AND RIGHT: Male cheetahs rigorously defend their territories, utilising scent marking and scratching of objects as part of this routine.

LEFT: Cheetahs are generally solitary animals: groups are usually mothers and offspring with the exception of coalitions formed by littermates.

OVERLEAF: A creature of the open savannah, the cheetah leads a relatively solitary life.

on the African savannah tend to spend most of the day sleeping and resting in the cooling shade of bushes and other cover, emerging to hunt and play again before dusk. Occasionally, cheetah will hunt after dark.

Communication between cheetahs takes many different forms. They are noticeably vocal and make a range of bird-like calls and dog-like 'yips'. Their calls can be heard by others for over 2km (1.2 miles) away and are used primarily as contact between females and young, or during greeting or courtship. Females will also use specific noises to instruct youngsters to stay put whilst she goes off hunting and during general social interactions. Cheetahs may also hiss, growl, snarl and purr as a part of their acoustic communications. Like our own domestic cats, they will purr loudly when content, during activities such as resting after feeding or when socialising with young.

Scent marking appears to be the main form of communication channel in cheetahs. They spend much time seeking out recently marked areas and objects, as well as scent marking these areas and objects themselves. Marking takes the form of carefully deposited urine or faeces, usually on a conspicuous object such as a tree or rock. Elevated levels are preferred, presumably because they facilitate the dispersal of volatile chemical signals in the urine.

Sniffing olfactory signals usually involves a cheetah crouching on its forelegs with its nose to the ground or marked area, in the presence of others it stimulates them to do the same. Both males and females urine mark, females increasing their frequency of doing so in the lead up to oestrus. Female faeces at this time are also known to be highly attractive to males. Defecation also occurs in prominent locations, such as elevations, termite mounds and boulders that are regularly visited by neighbouring cheetahs. These locations thus act as a form of smelly notice board to others.

At close quarters, the black teardrop markings on the cheetah's face accentuate subtle changes in facial expressions associated with mood or intentions. The rest of the cat's body is primarily designed for camouflage amongst the grasses of the savannah. However, from the rear the black spot markings on the ear tips are very conspicuous and

CHEETAH WATCHING

Masai Mara, Kenya

Masai Mara, Kenya

The cubs had now reached a crucial time in their lives, at nine months of age they had become used to finishing off their mother's kills and were becoming quite adventurous. We watched open-mouthed as we saw the trio, two brothers and a sister, focus their attention on an unsuspecting warthog trundling lazily past them, blissfully unaware that his every move was being eagerly assessed.

Warthogs are formidable opponents to most of the predators of the African savannah and even lions are reluctant to try their luck except with errant youngsters but these cubs simply couldn't resist and their natural instincts overtook them. Fascinated to see what would happen we sat patiently and watched hoping that the youngsters would not be injured in their pursuit of an animal with such a fearsome reputation.

Going through the typical stalking technique and then bursting into an explosive chase, the warthog squealed with surprise, turning on its heels and putting on an impressive turn of speed. The cubs soon gave up realising that they were out classed and out of breath long before the warthog stopped running.

Returning to the shade of a nearby bush they continued to watch and dream as the warthog, now fully aware of their presence, continued with his amble past them.

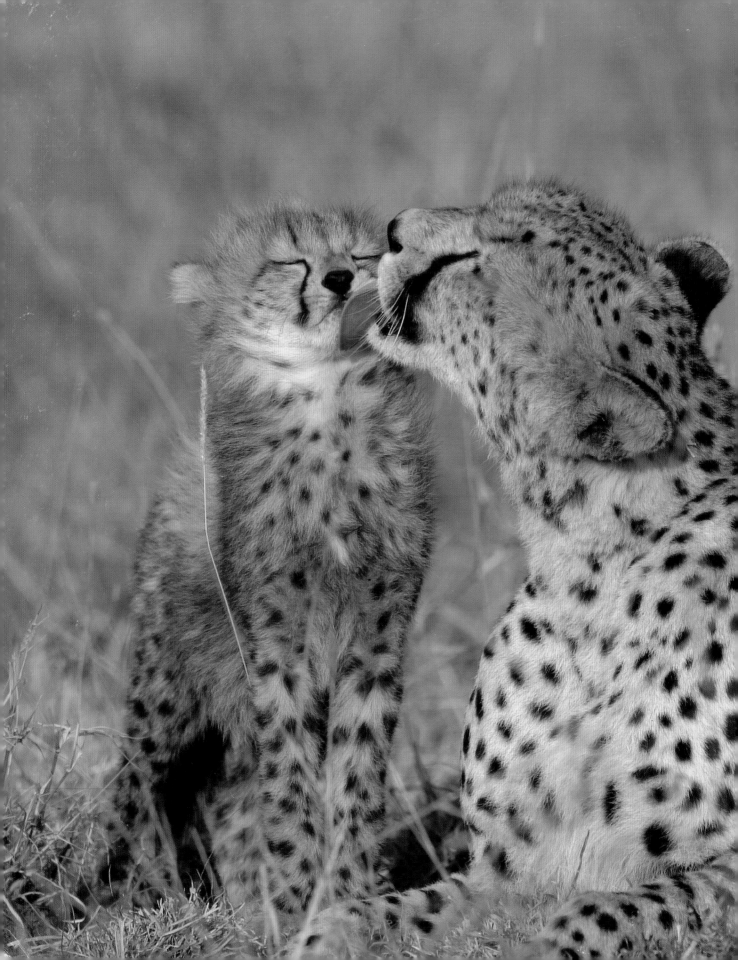

again are used to indicate subtleties in behavioural changes such as a readiness to hunt or worry caused by a competitor nearby. The tail being banded in black and white at the tip is also used as a form of visual communication. Experts speculate that its main role is to signal to others and perform a 'follow me' function to trailing offspring.

Tactile communication between individuals performs an important social function between females and their offspring, helping to strengthen the maternal bond. It also occurs between courting pairs and occasionally between close relatives when they meet. The main form of tactile communication between cheetahs is the 'greeting ceremony' where face licking, sniffing of mouth and genitals and cheek rubbing occurs much like that seen in domestic cats.

REPRODUCTION & GROWING UP

Female cheetahs become sexually active at around 22 months of age. Like many animals on the African plains, they do not have a specific breeding season and are able to breed at anytime. In spite of this, breeding activity usually coincides with the end of the rainy seasons, when their prey with also be giving birth. As a result, there tends to be a glut of potential prey items to sustain a hard-working, nursing mother and, later on, her hungry offspring.

Mating is an individual affair for cheetahs and may be prolonged or very brief. Females signal their receptivity through regular inspections of male scent marked areas in her home range; this is followed by counter marking of the site by herself. The male, the territory holder, upon meeting her, will make vocalisations which will entice the female towards him where he can copulate with her. During mating, the male will scruff the female at the back of her neck with his jaws. The female will spend much time grooming following copulation. Cheetahs are likely to copulate on several occasions

LEFT: Cheetahs dislike water, just like most other felines.

over the subsequent few hours or days. Further to this, the male and female disperse and the male plays no further part in the development and raising of his progeny.

Female cheetahs remain pregnant for between 90 - 95 days before giving birth in dense cover. The same or similar area is used to give birth in year after year.

Cheetah cubs - there are normally between 3 to 5 per litter - are born hidden in cover and are not exposed to the outside world until they are at least a month old. Born blind, cheetah cubs weigh between 150g – 300g (6-12oz). According to evidence gleaned from those bred in captivity, the cubs eyes open at around 10 days of age, they begin to walk at 16 days and their first teeth begin to appear at 20 days.

At around 5-6 weeks of age, cubs are given their first experience of a kill and they will then follow their mother wherever she goes. By the time they

FAR LEFT: Cheetah cubs can look as adorable to us as any domestic kitten.

LEFT AND ABOVE: Cubs are inquisitive from an early age and spend much time exploring their surroundings.

ABOVE TOP: A trio of cheetah cubs practising their running and chasing skills and (ABOVE) growing up is a tiring business.

RIGHT: A cheetah cub watches its siblings intently, ready to pounce.

are 3 months old, the cubs are experienced at sitting and waiting for their mother to go off and hunt. They remain hidden under a bush or motionless in long grass while the kill is in progress. Upon return, the mother will chirrup a call to encourage the cubs to come out of hiding and join in the feast. The cubs will run enthusiastically to greet her.

Unlike lions, there appears to be little direct competition between siblings for the food and so the meal is devoured quickly and quietly. This may

ABOVE: Cheetah cubs suckle from their mother regularly.

be a strategy for preventing any unwanted attention to themselves and/or their kill. In addition, at this stage of life, cubs will continue to suckle from their mother, gradually reducing their dependence on her milk as they are weaned onto a meat diet. After feeding, the mother cleans the cubs' faces by licking them. Again, it is assumed that this also acts to remove blood which may attract the attention of predators, whilst aiding in the development and strengthening social bonds between the family members. Further mutual grooming, usually accompanied by purring, is often stimulated by this behaviour.

Cheetah cubs are extremely vulnerable to predation by other big cats, such as lions and leopards, as well as by hyenas, baboons and wild dogs. It pays for them to remain as hidden as possible when in the vicinity of such creatures.

ABOVE, LEFT AND FAR LEFT: Cubs ensure that they watch everything going on in their surroundings.

ABOVE AND LEFT: Cheetah cubs remain within close proximity to their mother even when exploring and playing.

RIGHT: Even when a little older, cubs are interested in everything in their environment, including unsuspecting tortoises.

Their cryptic coat colour assists in hiding them in such situations, but the cheetah's best defence is to avoid these creatures and to keep on the move. Unlike their parents, cheetah cubs have a ridge of long fur, called a mantle, along their backs. It tends to be grey in colour. As well as providing a form of camouflage, it is also believed to resemble a honey badger or ratel (*Mellivora capensis*) which predators dislike due to its aggressive, fearless nature and tendency to excrete a foul-smelling fluid in defence.

From a very early age, cheetah cubs practice pouncing and running at their mother and siblings, biting their necks and tripping them. Cubs are curious about everything in their environment. They simulate their mother's hunting technique by climbing onto rocks and will regularly climb small bushes and trees. Precision hunting, which is essential to cheetah survival, is an art that needs plenty of practise, so cubs will attempt to stalk, chase and ambush each other, other animals and any inanimate objects they encounter.

At around 6 months of age, the female cheetah will begin to bring back prey that is temporarily disabled but not dead. She will release this in the

LEFT, BELOW AND RIGHT: Playing is an essential part of growing up in the life of a cheetah and is the only time when they can truly be described as social.

OVERLEAF: There is a life long bond between cheetah mothers and their cubs.

ABOVE: When there is no prey to practise upon, siblings will serve just as well.

LEFT: At six months, cheetah cubs begin lessons in hunting for themselves. Here, they try their skills against a baby Thomson gazelle.

RIGHT: Older cubs hone their running and chasing.

vicinity of the cubs for them to practice their hunting skills on. Small fawns and hares are fair game for the cubs by the time they reach 9 – 12 months of age but they are rarely able to kill the prey and are reliant on their mother to despatch the prey with a swift bite to the neck. Gradually, the cubs begin to be able to conduct a successful kill themselves at which time, the family is likely soon to disperse. At 18 months of age, the mother leaves the cubs, who then form a sibling group that will stay together for a further 6 months before separating and finding their own home range or territory.

LEFT: A sibling group will be left by their mother and will fend for themselves for up to 6 months before dispersing.

BELOW: Cubs remain with their mother until around 18 months to two years of age.

Studies in the Serengeti ecosystem (East Africa) have shown that up to 90 per cent of cheetah cubs may die in their first three months. The length of adult cheetah survival in the wild is unknown but in captivity lasts approximately 8-12 years. With such a fast-living survival strategy, they are unlikely to reach old age. Cheetahs that do not remain in optimum condition are likely to succumb to injury, disease, predators or starvation through an inability to hunt. Coupled to this the elimination of cheetahs in areas where they are tempted by prey such as domestic animals such as sheep, and their existing genetic problems of poor reproduction and the survival of a cheetah is a particularly difficult one.

MAN & CHEETAHS

We have had associations with cheetahs for many thousands of years. The ancient peoples of present day Iraq are the first to be documented as having kept them in captivity about 3,000 BC. Following this, a cat goddess (called Mafdet) was revered by the Egyptians and kept as companions to the pharoahs. Cheetah-like cats are depicted in Egyptian architecture and paintings, showing them as carriers of royal spirits to the after life.

The royal connection has been apparent throughout our relationship with cheetahs. From Ancient Egypt until at least the 16th century, cheetahs were used for sport hunting. This took the form of coursing, where the wild-caught cheetahs were released to chase game under a competitive situation. The possession of cheetahs in captivity became a symbol of status and it is known that nobility across the world, from Europe to China, would keep stables comprised of hundreds if not thousands of individual animals. Furthermore, there is only one historical record of a litter of cubs being born in captivity, which sadly did not survive. The harvesting of cheetahs from the wild and the lack of successful breeding in captivity had dire

RIGHT: The cheetahs survival in the twenty-first century is a precarious one.

86

consequences for the population remaining in the wild, especially in Asia. Today, the Asiatic cheetah is on the verge of extinction with only between 100-200 individuals surviving. The removal of cheetahs from the wild for a life in captivity continues to this day. Yet, even those found in zoological collections have poor reproductive success and are not self-sustaining.

The cheetah's survival in the 21st century is precarious. It has become one of the most highly specialised mammals on the planet. Through the process of evolution, it has sacrificed many of its wider adaptations such as strength and genetic diversity that would enable it to cope with changes in its environment. Extinction, over many millions of years, is a natural process but we have contributed to this with our booming global population and their associated demands on the world's resources. The effect is a new and radically accelerated rate of extinction with which other natural species have little chance to keep pace.

This, combined with the effects of a poor gene pool, means that cheetahs are vulnerable to human competition. The main causes of its current plight include the loss of natural habitat and prey through commercial farming and development; poaching and removal of

animals for captive purposes; and persecution by people believing that cheetahs pose a threat to their livestock.

The largest population of wild, free-ranging cheetah is found in Namibia: the second largest in East Africa. The cheetah population in Namibia comprises some 20 per cent (2500 cheetahs) of the world cheetah population and 90 per cent of these are found on farms outside of protected reserves, where they face increased competition from other predators, such as lions. On farms, lions and leopards have been removed and with access to water and a natural prey base, the cheetah has exploited this niche successfully. Despite this, from time to time, the Namibian habitat comes under pressure of drought and overgrazing by wild animals. Understandably, farmers reduce the pressures on the habitat and grazing by limiting the numbers of these prey animals which also sustain the cheetahs. Inevitably, with little natural food to eat, cheetahs are known to turn their attentions to domestic livestock. In turn, this leads to they themselves being hunted, thus exacerbating the critical situation the cheetah as a species is facing.

RIGHT: Conservation efforts are the cheetahs main hope of survival.

To conserve the cheetah as we know it today, we are dependent on the dedicated work of scientists to tease out the important aspects of cheetah life and its needs. Armed with this information they can then set about finding ways in which we can prevent further decline of this species, preserve what we have and - in the future - increase the numbers of cheetah in the wild, so that they may breed successfully and maintain a stable population.

The Cheetah Conservation Fund (CCF, www.cheetah.org) based in the Waterberg region of Namibia and led by scientist Dr Laurie Marker, is a project dedicated to the conservation of the world's remaining cheetah populations. CCF's goal is to help livestock farmers find ways to co-exist with cheetahs. They focus upon conducting research, education and the implementation of conservation management techniques in local communities and hope to achieve workable strategies that can then be employed throughout Africa. Creating sustainable cheetah populations in the wild is largely dependent on the willingness and capacity of individuals living alongside cheetahs.

In 1994. an innovative programme was launched to do just this — the Anatolian Shepherd Livestock Guarding programme. The Anatolian Shepherd dog has been bred for many thousands of years for guarding livestock in vast open areas in the absence of human guidance. Its job is to protect its herd of livestock from potential threats such as baboons, jackals, caracals, cheetahs, leopards and even humans. The dog is trained to bark and posture aggressively at the threat, thus scaring it away and/or alerting nearby humans to its presence. Occasionally, the dog will be forced to defend its herd physically, its size and strength making this a formidable opponent.

In Namibia, the climate is very similar to that on the Anatolian plateau in Turkey where the breed originates. It sustains extreme   heat and little rain at times coupled with severe cold in winter. The Anatolian Shepherd dog has a sandy-coloured coat and dark facial markings. The coat insulates the dog against extreme temperatures and the effects of the harsh African sun. Standing at over 60.9 cm (24in) at the shoulder and weighing 70.3 — 74.8kg (155-165lb), they are big imposing dogs ideally suited to their job.

RIGHT: The Cheetah Conservation Fund in Namibia is helping to conserve cheetahs alongside human activity..

CCF have in place a selective breeding programme for these dogs. Pups are exposed to their herd at the age of 7-8 weeks of age. With minimal human contact they develop a bond with the livestock, living, eating and sleeping alongside their charges. They are gradually introduced to the dangers of the African bush (such as snakes and predators), and eventually are placed with carefully selected farmers. The farmers are further trained in how to care for their dogs. From an initial 10 dogs imported from the United States, today there are over 80 dogs at work on Namibian farms protecting livestock herds and thus improving the potential for cheetah survival.

It is by supporting the research and active conservation programmes such as those championed by CCF that we may, in time, be able to save the cheetah from extinction and ensure that this most specialised of big cats remains in viable numbers in the wild for future generations to come. As human beings we are directly responsible for the accelerated decline of this species and it is therefore up to us to make sure that we are not responsible for its ultimate extinction from the Earth.

ACKNOWLEDGEMENTS & INFORMATION

A great many people deserve specific thanks for their help in the production of this book including PVV and Prof T; John Njenga ; Isaack Ntari ; Nancy, Theo and Mike at the Mara Safari Club; Dr Laurie Marker and all at CCF; Carla Conradie; Maria and Jorg Diekmann; Andrew Momberg; Greg and Wendy Trollip; the good company we shared on our safaris (Ian, Marion, Chris, Frank, Nathalie, Jonathan, Emma, Andy and Phil); Sunita Gahir and of course the subjects of this book, the cheetahs, without whom the world would be a far less fascinating place.

WHERE TO STAY TO SEE CHEETAHS

Kenya
Mara Safari Club, Masai Mara
Located at the foot of the Aitong Hills in the north west of the Masai Mara, the camp is positioned on an ox-bow of the Mara River, so that all en-suite tents (50) have a view of the hippo-filled river.
The luxurious tents are erected on a concrete plinth and each have a game-viewing verandah.

E: sales@lonrhohotels.co.ke | W: www.lonrhohotels.com
T: (254 020) 216940 | Best times to visit: Jan — Mar and Aug — Nov

Tanzania
Serengeti Serena Safari Lodge
Set high on the saddle of tree-clad ridge commanding panoramic views over the endlessly rolling Serengeti wherein is enacted the thunderous theatre of the million-strong wildebeest migration.
The Lodge features thickly-thatched, stone-built rooms, spaciously set amongst groves of indigenous trees that are cooled by sparkling streams and papyrus-fringed ponds.

W: www.serenahotels.com | Best times to visit: Jan — Mar and Aug — Nov

Namibia
Cheetah Conservation Fund, Otjiwarongo
CCF's focus is on research, conservation and education. An extensive modern Visitor and Education Centre encourages visitors to learn about cheetahs, their habitat and issues of conservation, with an opportunity to see resident non-releasable cheetahs, acting as 'cheetah ambassadors' for the species. CCF is open daily from 9am-5pm. Visitors can also observe cheetahs being fed (most afternoons except Sundays around 2.30pm, and at noon on Saturdays), and meet staff who will show them around the centre and answer questions. As a not-for-profit Trust, CCF funds its research and its education activities entirely from donations, therefore, a minimum donation of N$60 per person is expected for your visit. (N = Namibian dollars)

W: www.cheetah.org | E: info@cheetah.org
T: +1 (805) 640-0390 | Best times to visit: any time

Okonjima, Otjiwarongo (meaning the place of the baboons)
Luxury camp and bush camp comprise ten en-suite double rooms, three twin bed tents and eight thatched chalets. Also home of the Africat foundation, a non-profit making conservation effort supporting a range of big cat programmes in the area. Visit the rehabilitation areas and see cheetahs at close hand.

T: 264 (0) 67 304563 / 4 | E: okonjima@iway.na or info@okonjima.com | W: www.okonjima.com
Best times to visit: any time

Name of Photo: Full speed ahead

Page: 9

No book on Cheetahs would be complete without high action shots. The major challenge was to keep the speeding cheetah in the camera's viewfinder. All focusing points were selected and the autofocus set to tracking AI servo. Keeping the aperture wide open we would be shooting at the maximum shutter speed possible. (Canon EOS 1V HS, Canon 500mm F4L lens, Fuji Provia 100F pushed to 200, exposure 1/1000th sec. at f4)

Name of Photo: Soggy cats

Page: 68/69

Sometimes the worst weather can yield great pictures. We sat through 80mm of rain in an hour with this family of cheetah and, from our knowledge of animal behaviour, knew that they would soon shake themselves dry as soon as it relented. As the light level was quite low we increased the ISO setting to 160; it is a fine line between retaining image quality and getting enough shutter speed to freeze the moment but we hit this one spot on (Canon EOS 1Ds, Canon 500mm F4L IS lens with 1.4x teleconverter, exposure 1/320th sec. at f5.6).

Name of Photo: Royal glow

Page: 56/57

Backlit shots only work when the sun is close to the horizon as the red highlight is only visible at this brief moment. When shooting backlit shots there are always two options - shoot the subject totally in silhouette or retain some detail of the subject. The low light level caused a low shutter speed and increased risk of so to camera shake. To combat this we used an image-stabilised lens and an off-camera release cord. (Canon EOS 1D, Canon 500mm F4L IS lens, exposure 1/50th sec. at f4, ISO 200)

Name of Photo: Cub portrait in tree

Page: 70

Composition of an image can be all important when trying to tell the story of it. With this cute image of a young cub, we deliberately offset it to the right to ensure that the paw remained visible. We also resisted the temptation to take a frame filling shot, as that would have cropped out the reason for the cub being there which was that it was playing in the tree. One of the advantages of using a digital SLR is that on gloomy, overcast days like this one, our images are bright and alive. (Canon EOS 1Ds, Canon 500mm F4L IS lens with 1.4x teleconverter, exposure 1/125th sec. at f5.6, ISO 50)

Name of Photo: Snarler

Page: cover and 58

Moments like this image of a cheetah snarling only happen fleetingly and being familiar with the camera is vital to capturing the shot. We know how to adjust every control on the camera by touch alone, which means that we can keep our eye where it should be — looking through the viewfinder. When the cheetah snarled we quickly selected the focusing point just above centre so that the point of focus would be right between the eyes. (Canon EOS 1Ds, Canon 500mm F4L IS lens, exposure 1/250th sec at f4, ISO 50).